Don't just teach me, show me how to make it in this world

Bernard H. Jones, Jr

ACKNOWLEDGMENT

I offer my sincerest gratitude to God, who has been my rock and spiritual leader. Without his guidance and support, I am nothing, but with him, I am everything.

I extend my heartfelt appreciation to Evie Rodriguez and the late Dr. Louise Gibney for their timeless consultation, collaboration, and reflection. Dr. Gibney's wisdom and insights continue to inspire me, and her passing leaves a void that cannot be filled.

I am forever indebted to my father, the late Bernard H. Jones, Sr., and my mother, Geraldine C. Jones, my brother Rev. Cornell Jones, and my sister, Hylene Jones-Pankey, for their unwavering belief in me. They equipped me with the tools necessary to navigate this world, and their legacy lives on in my journey.

To my beloved children, Bernard H. Jones, III, and Ashley L. Jones, I am immensely proud of the individuals you have become. Your resilience and determination assure me that you will thrive in this world and continue to make a positive impact.

These acknowledgments are a testament to the invaluable support and love that have surrounded me throughout this journey.

TABLE OF CONTENTS

Introduction... 1

Chapter 1 Mastering Your Finances................................. 8

Chapter 2 The Art of Negotiation 31

Chapter 3 Communicate with Impact 46

Chapter 4 Cultivating Positive Mindsets 62

Chapter 5 Building Resilience in Adversity.................... 73

Chapter 6 Nurturing Social and Emotional Intelligence.............. 82

Chapter 7 The Practice of Mindfulness 95

Embracing Your Journey... 104

INTRODUCTION

In a world where challenges can seem insurmountable, where the path to success can feel like an endless maze, one question echoes louder than any other: How do we make it? How do we carve our place in this vast, ever-changing world?

This book, "Don't Just Teach Me, Show Me How to Make It in This World," is born from a deeply personal journey and a profound sense of responsibility. As the son of the late, Bernard H. Jones, Sr, a man who dedicated his life to creating opportunities for African Americans and others, I carry with me a legacy of empowerment and service. My father's tireless efforts to establish programs for underserved communities ignited within me a passion to continue his work, to reach out a helping hand to those who face the same challenges he sought to overcome.

In the pages that follow, I aim to address the pressing issues that continue to hinder the progress of African Americans and indeed, many others, in today's world. From the persistent specter of racial inequalities to the daunting task of navigating a complex web of information, from the fragility of economic foundations to the urgent need for more diverse and relatable role models, these challenges loom large, casting long shadows over the aspirations of millions.

Through personal anecdotes and shared experiences, we will explore the multifaceted nature of these obstacles, delving into the heart of the matter with honesty and empathy. From the struggle to distinguish between assets and liabilities to the imperative of self-care in the face of mounting health concerns, each chapter is a testament to the resilience and determination of those who refuse to be defined by their circumstances.

As we embark on this journey together, my hope is not only to shed light on the challenges we face but also to illuminate the path forward. Drawing upon the wisdom of our ancestors and the lessons of our shared history, we will uncover strategies for success, forging a new narrative of empowerment and possibility.

This book is not just a collection of words on a page; it is a call to action, an invitation to join hands and build a brighter future for ourselves and generations to come.

In the pursuit of progress and prosperity, education has long been heralded as the great equalizer, the key to unlocking doors previously closed to us. Yet, as we journey through the corridors of academia, we come to realize that traditional measures of success can only take us so far. It is not enough to simply accumulate knowledge; we must also learn how to apply it, how to navigate the complexities of the world beyond the classroom.

This realization forms the cornerstone of our exploration in this book. We delve beyond the confines of conventional education and testing, recognizing that true empowerment lies not in rote memorization but in the cultivation of practical skills that empower us to thrive in every aspect of our lives.

For African Americans, the stakes are particularly high. We are not only striving to build ourselves up educationally and economically but also collaboratively and spiritually, forging pathways to success that honor our heritage and uplift our communities.

Through these pages, we aim to provide a roadmap for this journey, offering insights and strategies that address the specific needs and struggles faced by African Americans. By cultivating critical thinking skills, teaching problem-solving techniques, and imparting budgeting and money management know-how, we equip ourselves with the tools necessary to navigate the complexities of the modern world.

But our journey does not end there. We must also learn how to analyze and evaluate ideas, how to synthesize and evaluate information, honing our abilities to discern truth from falsehood and chart our own course in a sea of uncertainty.

By embracing a holistic approach to success, we aim to cultivate a mindset of collaboration and community, encouraging readers to reach out and connect with others in pursuit of common goals. Through ongoing collaboration, we can harness the power of collective action, pooling our resources and talents to effect meaningful change in our lives and communities.

Moreover, this book seeks to promote sustainability in all its forms, from environmentally conscious practices to socially responsible initiatives that uplift and empower those in need. By promoting sustainable activities, we not only safeguard the planet for future generations but also create opportunities for economic growth and social progress that benefit us all.

Central to our approach is the emphasis on networking, recognizing that the strength of our connections can often determine the breadth of our opportunities. By developing meaningful relationships with others, we expand our horizons, opening doors to new possibilities and forging partnerships that propel us toward our goals.

But perhaps most importantly, this book advocates for grassroots activism and advocacy, empowering readers to become agents of change in their own communities. By championing causes close to their hearts and speaking out against injustice, individuals can make a tangible impact on the world around them, leaving a legacy of compassion and courage for future generations to inherit.

What sets this approach apart from other self-help books addressing similar topics is its departure from the traditional paradigm of success. Rather than adhering to a rigid formula of hard work and academic achievement, we embrace a more nuanced understanding of success—one rooted in relationships, collaboration, balance, networking, and belief systems.

Throughout the book, the readers will go through a diverse array of themes and topics aimed at empowering individuals to lead meaningful and purposeful lives. One overarching theme centers on leading a life infused with intention and purpose, delving into the significance of aligning personal values with overarching life goals. Additionally, the exploration of African American identity serves as a cornerstone, acknowledging the complexities of identity formation within the context of contemporary society while celebrating cultural heritage and navigating issues of race and identity. Physical education and self-care are also prominently featured, emphasizing the critical role of physical health and well-being in overall happiness and success, and providing practical strategies for integrating exercise, nutrition, and self-care practices into daily routines.

Furthermore, the transformative power of reading takes center stage, as readers are invited to explore the cognitive, emotional, and social benefits of regular reading habits. From spiritual needs to the exploration of different spiritual practices and traditions within the African American community, the book provides insights into nurturing spiritual well-being and finding inner peace amidst life's challenges. Finally, a comprehensive business directory and personal development guide offer readers access to essential services and resources for holistic growth, covering topics ranging from healthcare and education to financial literacy and emotional intelligence.

As we come to the end of this introduction, I want to emphasize how this journey ahead is tailored specifically for you – members of the African American community. We've talked about important topics like finding your purpose, taking care of yourself, and embracing your identity in a world that sometimes doesn't fully understand it.

But don't worry, we're just scratching the surface. In the upcoming chapters, we'll delve deeper into these themes, providing practical advice and resources to help you navigate the unique challenges and opportunities you face. Whether it's improving your health, connecting with your cultural roots, or honing your skills for success, this book is here to support you every step of the way.

So get ready to embark on this journey with us. Together, we'll explore, learn, and grow, discovering just how resilient and capable you truly are. Welcome to "Don't Just Teach Me, Show Me How to Make It in This World," a book crafted specifically for the African American community. Let's dive in and explore together!

CHAPTER 1

MASTERING YOUR FINANCES

Mastering your finances is a critical skill that can significantly impact your overall well-being and quality of life. Imagine a scenario where two individuals, let's call them Alex and Emily, both graduate from college with similar degrees and career aspirations. However, their approach to managing their finances differs drastically.

Alex, despite earning a decent salary, has little knowledge of financial literacy. He spend impulsively, often splurging on unnecessary purchases and living paycheck to paycheck. As a result, Alex finds himself drowning in debt, unable to save for the future, and constantly stressed about money.

On the other hand, Emily has taken the time to educate herself about financial literacy. She understands the importance of budgeting, saving, and investing wisely. Emily creates a detailed budget, tracks her expenses diligently, and prioritizes saving for emergencies and long-term goals.

Now, let's fast forward a few years into the future. Despite starting in similar financial situations, Emily has achieved a level of economic self-sufficiency that Alex can only dream of. She has built a robust emergency fund, contributed regularly to retirement accounts, and even managed to purchase her own home. Emily feels financially secure, empowered, and confident in her ability to navigate life's uncertainties.

Meanwhile, Alex continues to struggle with debt and financial instability. The stress of living paycheck to paycheck takes a toll on their mental and emotional well-being, affecting their relationships and overall happiness.

This example highlights the crucial importance of mastering your finances. Whether it's understanding financial literacy, creating and sticking to a budget, or saving and investing for the future, taking control of your financial situation can pave the way to a more secure and fulfilling life. Throughout this chapter, we will explore these topics in more detail, providing practical tips and insights to help you achieve financial mastery and economic self-sufficiency. Let's embark on this journey together towards a brighter financial future.

Understanding Financial Literacy:

Financial literacy may sound like a complex concept, but at its core, it's simply about having the knowledge and skills to make smart choices with your money. Think of it as your roadmap to financial success, guiding you through the twists and turns of budgeting, saving, investing, and more.

At its essence, financial literacy means knowing how to manage your finances in a responsible and effective way. It's about understanding the basics of personal finance, like creating a budget, tracking your expenses, and saving for the future. But it's also about having the confidence to navigate more complex financial matters, like investing in the stock market or planning for retirement.

Imagine financial literacy as a toolbox filled with valuable resources to help you build a solid financial foundation. Inside, you'll find tools for budgeting, tools for saving, and tools for investing. Each tool serves a different purpose, but together, they empower you to take control of your financial future.

Financial literacy is not just about knowing how to manage your own money; it's also about understanding how money works in the world around you. It's about being able to read and interpret financial statements, understand the terms of a loan or credit card agreement, and make informed decisions about your financial future.

Ultimately, financial literacy is the key to financial empowerment. When you have a solid understanding of how to manage your money effectively, you're better equipped to achieve your financial goals, whether that's buying a home, starting a business, or saving for retirement. So take the time to invest in your financial education – it's an investment that will pay dividends for years to come.

The Importance of Economic Self-Sufficiency:

Achieving economic self-sufficiency is more than just a financial goal; it's a pathway to freedom and security. When you are economically self-sufficient, you have the power to control your financial destiny, paving the way for a life of independence and prosperity. Let's explore why economic self-sufficiency is so important and how it can transform your financial future.

1. Controls what comes in and what goes out:

Economic self-sufficiency puts you in the driver's seat of your finances. You have the ability to determine your income streams and manage your expenses effectively. By controlling what comes in (income) and what goes out (expenses), you can create a balanced financial picture that aligns with your goals and priorities.

2. Budgeting without depending on others:

One of the hallmarks of economic self-sufficiency is the ability to budget effectively without relying on others for financial support. Instead of living paycheck to paycheck or relying on loans or handouts, you have the skills and resources to create a budget that works for you. This independence not only promotes financial stability but also instills a sense of pride and confidence in your ability to manage your own finances.

3. Distinguish between asset and liability:

Economic self-sufficiency goes beyond simply earning money; it's about understanding the difference between assets and liabilities and leveraging this knowledge to build wealth. Assets are things that put money in your pocket, like investments or income-generating properties, while liabilities are things that take money out of your pocket, like debt or unnecessary expenses. By distinguishing between the two, you can make informed decisions that contribute to your long-term financial success.

4. Can save you money by controlling what's coming in and what's going out:

When you're economically self-sufficient, you're better equipped to save money by controlling your income and expenses. By being mindful of your spending habits and prioritizing saving and investing, you can build a financial cushion that protects you from unexpected expenses or downturns in the economy. This proactive approach to money management can ultimately save you money in the long run and provide greater financial security.

5. Helps with money sense - distinguishing between what's credible vs. scams:

Economic self-sufficiency also involves developing a keen sense of financial literacy, which enables you to distinguish between credible opportunities and scams. With a solid understanding of personal finance principles, you can spot red flags, ask the right questions, and make informed decisions about where to invest your time and money. This critical thinking skills not only protects you from falling victim to scams but also empowers you to make choices that align with your financial goals and values.

Financial literacy is more than just a buzzword; it's a fundamental aspect of personal empowerment and economic stability. However, the lack of financial literacy can have dire consequences, leading to financial insecurity and mounting debt. In this section, we will explore how the absence of financial literacy contributes to these challenges and the potential pitfalls individuals may encounter.

1. Lack of control:

Without a basic understanding of financial principles, individuals may find themselves feeling powerless over their financial situation. They may struggle to create and stick to a budget, fail to track their expenses effectively, and feel overwhelmed by financial decisions. This lack of control can lead to a sense of helplessness and contribute to ongoing financial insecurity.

2. Could cost you thousands:

The absence of financial literacy can result in costly mistakes. From high-interest debt to missed investment opportunities, the financial repercussions of uninformed decisions can be significant. Without the knowledge to make informed choices, individuals may inadvertently waste money on unnecessary fees, penalties, or interest payments, ultimately costing them thousands over time.

3. Hurt you as being a consumer:

Financial illiteracy can leave individuals vulnerable to exploitation and manipulation as consumers. Without the ability to distinguish between credible financial products and scams, individuals may fall victim to predatory lending practices, fraudulent investment schemes, or deceptive marketing tactics. This can lead to devastating financial losses and erode trust in the financial system.

4. Bank fees:

One common consequence of financial illiteracy is the accumulation of unnecessary bank fees. From overdraft charges to ATM fees, individuals who are unaware of how to manage their accounts effectively may incur avoidable expenses. These fees can quickly add up, further exacerbating financial insecurity and making it harder to break free from the cycle of debt.

Financial literacy is not just about knowing how to balance a checkbook or create a budget. It encompasses a wide range of concepts and skills that are essential for navigating the complex world of personal finance. From making informed investment decisions to understanding the intricacies of credit scores and loans, financial literacy empowers individuals to take control of their financial futures.

1. Good vs. Bad Investments:

One of the fundamental aspects of financial literacy is the ability to distinguish between good and bad investments. This involves understanding the risks and potential returns associated with different investment opportunities, such as stocks, bonds, real estate, and mutual funds. Being able to evaluate investment options critically allows individuals to make informed decisions that align with their financial goals and risk tolerance.

2. Credit Score:

A credit score is a numerical representation of an individual's creditworthiness, which plays a crucial role in various financial transactions, including applying for loans, renting an apartment, or even getting a job. Financial literacy involves understanding how credit scores are calculated, how they can impact financial opportunities, and how to maintain a healthy credit profile.

3. Loans:

Loans are a common financial tool used to finance major purchases, such as homes, cars, or education. Financial literacy includes knowledge about the different types of loans available, their terms and conditions, and the implications of taking on debt. Understanding loans empowers individuals to make responsible borrowing decisions and manage debt effectively.

4. Retirement:

Planning for retirement is a critical aspect of financial literacy. It involves understanding retirement savings vehicles, such as employer-sponsored 401(k) plans, individual retirement accounts (IRAs), and pension plans. Financially literate individuals are equipped to set retirement goals, estimate future expenses, and develop strategies to build a nest egg that will support them in their golden years.

5. Savings:

Saving money is a fundamental component of financial literacy. It involves developing the habit of setting aside a portion of income for future needs and emergencies. Financially literate individuals understand the importance of saving regularly, establishing emergency funds, and prioritizing long-term goals, such as homeownership, education, or travel.

6. Economics:

A basic understanding of economic principles is essential for making informed financial decisions. Financial literacy includes knowledge about concepts such as supply and demand, inflation, interest rates, and economic cycles. Understanding economics provides individuals with valuable insights into the broader economic environment and how it can impact their personal finances.

7. Statistics:

Statistics play a crucial role in financial decision-making, particularly when it comes to assessing risk and evaluating investment opportunities. Financial literacy involves understanding basic statistical concepts, such as probability, standard deviation, and correlation. This knowledge allows individuals to analyze financial data effectively and make sound investment decisions based on evidence and analysis.

Budgeting Basics:

Budgeting is a fundamental skill that forms the cornerstone of financial success. It's about more than just tracking your expenses – it's about taking control of your money and making intentional decisions about how you want to spend it. For the African American community, budgeting can be especially empowering, providing a pathway to financial stability and generational wealth.

At its core, budgeting involves creating a plan for how you will allocate your income to cover your expenses and meet your financial goals. Here are some simple steps to help you master budgeting basics:

1. Start by tracking your income:

Calculate how much money you earn each month from all sources, including salaries, wages, and any additional income streams.

2. List your expenses:

Make a comprehensive list of all your monthly expenses, including rent or mortgage payments, utilities, groceries, transportation, and discretionary spending like entertainment and dining out.

3. Differentiate between needs and wants:

Distinguish between essential expenses that are necessary for survival (needs) and non-essential expenses that are desirable but not crucial (wants). This will help you prioritize your spending and identify areas where you can cut back if needed.

4. Set financial goals:

Establish short-term and long-term financial goals, such as building an emergency fund, paying off debt, saving for a home, or investing for retirement. Having clear goals will guide your budgeting decisions and keep you motivated.

5. Allocate your income:

Once you've identified your income and expenses, allocate your income to cover your needs first, then allocate funds towards your wants and savings goals. Aim to spend less than you earn and prioritize saving and investing for the future.

6. Monitor and adjust:

Regularly review your budget to track your spending and ensure that you're staying on track with your financial goals. Be flexible and willing to adjust your budget as your financial situation or priorities change.

Now, let's illustrate these budgeting basics with an example:

Imagine Jamal, a young professional in the African American community, wants to take control of his finances and build a secure future for himself and his family. Jamal starts by tracking his monthly income, which amounts to $3,000 from his job. He then lists his expenses, including $1,200 for rent, $200 for utilities, $400 for groceries, $200 for transportation, $100 for entertainment, and $100 for savings.

After differentiating between his needs and wants, Jamal realizes that he can cut back on his entertainment expenses and allocate more towards his savings goal. He decides to reduce his entertainment budget to $50 and increase his savings contribution to $150.

By following these budgeting basics, Jamal is able to prioritize his spending, save for the future, and achieve his financial goals, setting himself on the path to financial success and prosperity.

Remember, budgeting is a powerful tool that can help you take control of your finances and achieve your dreams. By mastering these budgeting basics, you can pave the way to a brighter financial future for yourself and your community.

Tracking expenses and staying accountable within a budget are essential components of effective financial management. Without a clear understanding of where your money is going, it's challenging to make informed decisions and stay on track with your financial goals. Fortunately, there are practical tips and strategies that can help you track your expenses and hold yourself accountable within your budget.

1. Write it down:

One of the most effective ways to track your expenses is to write them down or use a digital budgeting tool. Keep a record of every dollar you spend, whether it's on groceries, utilities, or discretionary purchases like dining out or entertainment. By documenting your expenses, you gain insight into your spending habits and can identify areas where you may be overspending.

2. Be accountable for everything spent – keep a log:

Maintain a detailed log of your expenses to hold yourself accountable within your budget. This could be as simple as jotting down each purchase in a notebook or using a budgeting app to track your spending electronically. The key is to record every expense as soon as it occurs, ensuring that you have an accurate picture of your financial habits.

3. Reflect on expenses on a regular basis:

Take time to review your expenses regularly to assess your progress towards your financial goals and identify any areas for improvement. Reflect on your spending habits and consider whether your purchases align with your priorities and values. This reflection allows you to make adjustments to your budget as needed and stay accountable for your financial decisions.

4. Determine how you could save money:

As you track your expenses, look for opportunities to save money and reduce unnecessary spending. Identify areas where you can cut back or find more cost-effective alternatives without sacrificing your quality of life. Whether its meal prepping at home instead of dining out or canceling unused subscriptions, small changes can add up to significant savings over time.

5. Set goals:

Setting clear financial goals can help you stay motivated and focused on your budgeting efforts. Whether you're saving for a down payment on a house, paying off debt, or building an emergency fund, having specific goals gives you a sense of purpose and direction. Break down your goals into smaller, achievable milestones and track your progress regularly to celebrate your successes and stay motivated.

Prioritizing spending within a budget is essential for ensuring that you're allocating your resources towards the most important aspects of your life while staying within your financial means. By implementing effective strategies, you can make intentional decisions about where your money goes, ensuring that you're meeting your needs and working towards your financial goals. Here are some practical tips for prioritizing spending within a budget:

1. Needs before wants:

When making purchasing decisions, prioritize your needs over your wants. Focus on covering essential expenses such as housing, utilities, groceries, and transportation before allocating funds towards discretionary spending like entertainment or luxury items. By meeting your basic needs first, you ensure that your essential expenses are covered before indulging in non-essential purchases.

2. Reward yourself:

While it's important to prioritize your needs, it's also essential to incorporate some flexibility and enjoyment into your budget. Consider allocating a portion of your budget towards discretionary spending or personal rewards as a way to motivate yourself and maintain a healthy balance between financial responsibility and enjoyment. Setting aside funds for occasional treats or leisure activities can help you stay motivated and avoid feeling deprived.

3. Write it down and reflect regularly:

Keep track of your spending by writing down every purchase you make and regularly reviewing your expenses against your budget. This allows you to stay accountable and identify areas where you may be overspending or where you can cut back. By reflecting on your spending habits regularly, you can make adjustments as needed to ensure that your spending aligns with your priorities and financial goals.

Saving and Investing:

Understanding the distinctions between saving and investing is essential for building a solid financial foundation and achieving long-term financial stability. While both saving and investing involve setting aside money for future use, they serve different purposes and offer unique benefits. Let's delve into the differences between saving and investing, and why both are crucial for securing your financial future.

Saving:

Saving involves setting aside money for short-term goals, emergencies, and unexpected expenses. It's about creating a financial safety net to cover immediate needs and protect against financial setbacks. Savings are typically held in accessible and low-risk accounts, such as savings accounts, money market accounts, or certificates of deposit (CDs). The primary goal of saving is to preserve capital and ensure liquidity, making funds readily available when needed.

Investing:

Investing, on the other hand, is about growing your wealth over the long term by putting your money to work for you. Unlike savings, which focus on preserving capital, investing involves taking calculated risks in pursuit of higher returns. Investments may include a wide range of assets, such as stocks, bonds, real estate, mutual funds, retirement accounts (e.g., 401(k), 403(b)), and precious metals. The goal of investing is to generate income and achieve capital appreciation over time, leveraging the power of compound interest and market growth.

Why Both are Important:

Both saving and investing play complementary roles in achieving long-term financial stability and success. Here's why:

1. Financial Security:

Savings provide a safety net for emergencies and unexpected expenses, ensuring that you have funds readily available to cover immediate needs without resorting to debt or liquidating investments. Investing, on the other hand, offers the potential for long-term wealth accumulation and financial growth, helping you build a nest egg for the future and achieve your financial goals.

2. Diversification:

Saving and investing allow you to diversify your financial portfolio, spreading risk across different asset classes and investment vehicles. While savings provide stability and liquidity, investments offer growth potential and the opportunity to generate passive income. By diversifying your financial assets, you can mitigate risk and optimize returns, enhancing overall financial resilience.

3. Wealth Building:

Saving and investing work together to build wealth over time. Savings provide the foundation for investing, allowing you to accumulate the initial capital needed to start investing and take advantage of opportunities for growth. By consistently saving and investing over the long term, you can harness the power of compounding and asset appreciation to steadily increase your net worth and achieve financial independence.

Saving money, regardless of income level, is a crucial step towards achieving financial stability and reaching your long-term financial goals. While it may seem challenging, especially for individuals with limited income, there are several effective strategies that can help you save money and build a financial safety net. Let's explore these strategies in detail:

1. Set goals:

Setting specific, achievable savings goals is the first step towards successful money management. Whether you're saving for an emergency fund, a major purchase, or retirement, having clear goals provides motivation and direction for your saving efforts. Break down your goals into smaller, manageable targets, and establish a timeline for reaching each milestone. This will help you stay focused and track your progress over time.

2. Pay yourself first:

One of the most effective savings strategies is to prioritize saving by paying yourself first. Treat your savings like a non-negotiable expense and allocate a portion of your income towards savings before paying your bills or spending on discretionary items. Consider setting up automatic transfers from your checking account to your savings account on payday to ensure that savings are consistently prioritized. By making saving a priority, you'll build a habit of regular saving and accumulate funds over time.

3. See how you can trim expenses:

Take a close look at your expenses and identify areas where you can cut back or reduce costs. Look for opportunities to trim unnecessary spending, such as dining out less frequently, canceling unused subscriptions or memberships, or finding cheaper alternatives for everyday purchases. Be mindful of your spending habits and prioritize needs over wants. Every dollar saved can contribute to your savings goals and increase your financial security.

4. Keep your eyes on the item you're interested in:

Stay focused on your savings goals and remain committed to your financial objectives. Visualize the item or outcome you're saving for, whether it's a dream vacation, a new car, or a debt-free future. Keeping your goals in mind will help you resist temptation and stay motivated to save, even when faced with financial challenges or unexpected expenses. Consider creating a visual reminder, such as a vision board or savings thermometer, to track your progress and celebrate milestones along the way.

Overcoming Financial Obstacles:

Overcoming significant financial challenges often begins with identifying the root cause of the problem and taking proactive steps to address it. One common obstacle many individuals face is the feeling of financial uncertainty, where it seems like money is slipping away without a clear understanding of where it's going. This was precisely the dilemma I found myself in not too long ago. Despite earning a steady income, it felt like my finances were spiraling out of control, with each month bringing less financial stability than the last. Determined to regain control of my financial situation, I embarked on a journey of tracking my expenses meticulously.

As I began tracking every penny spent, a remarkable transformation occurred. What initially seemed like an arduous task soon became a liberating experience. By holding myself accountable for each expenditure, I gained valuable insights into my spending habits and financial behaviors. It was eye-opening to realize that while I made the same amount of money each month, I had been unknowingly frittering it away on unnecessary purchases and frivolous expenses.

The turning point came when I recognized that just as law firms, schools, banks, and government institutions operate within budgets to maintain financial stability, I too needed to adopt a similar approach. Armed with this newfound realization, I embraced the principles of budgeting and financial discipline wholeheartedly.

By establishing a budget and adhering to it rigorously, I not only regained control over my finances but also discovered newfound financial freedom. With each passing month, I watched in amazement as my savings grew and my financial worries diminished. The simple act of tracking expenses and embracing accountability proved to be the catalyst for a profound transformation in my financial life.

This personal anecdote serves as a testament to the power of taking control of one's finances and holding oneself accountable for every penny spent. By recognizing the importance of budgeting and adopting financial discipline, I was able to overcome a significant financial challenge and pave the way towards a brighter financial future.

As we conclude this chapter, remember that mastering your finances is a journey, not a destination. It requires ongoing education, discipline, and commitment to financial well-being. By embracing the principles and strategies discussed in this chapter, you're taking a crucial step towards financial empowerment and creating a brighter future for yourself and your loved ones.

In the next chapter, we'll delve into the art of negotiation, exploring principles and techniques for effective communication and conflict resolution. Stay tuned as we continue our journey towards personal and financial growth.

CHAPTER 2

THE ART OF NEGOTIATION

Negotiation is a skill that transcends boundaries and empowers individuals to navigate life's challenges with confidence and resilience. In the African American community, negotiation plays a pivotal role in advocating for equal opportunities, advancing career aspirations, and achieving economic empowerment. Whether negotiating salaries, contracts, or resolving conflicts, mastering the art of negotiation is essential for success in both personal and professional realms.

Consider the story of Malik, a young African American professional striving to climb the corporate ladder. Despite his qualifications and hard work, Malik finds himself facing disparities in pay and opportunities compared to his peers. Frustrated by the systemic barriers he encounters, Malik realizes the importance of honing his negotiation skills to level the playing field and advocate for himself effectively.

Malik's journey mirrors the experiences of many within the African American community, where negotiation serves as a tool for empowerment and social change. From historic civil rights movements to contemporary workplace negotiations, African Americans have long recognized the power of negotiation in challenging inequities and achieving progress.

In this chapter, we'll explore the principles of negotiation and practical techniques for success, drawing from the rich legacy of African American leaders and advocates. Through personal anecdotes, case studies, and actionable strategies, we'll uncover the art of negotiation and empower readers to navigate life's challenges with confidence and conviction. Join us as we embark on a journey towards mastering the art of negotiation and unlocking boundless opportunities for personal and collective advancement.

Principles of Negotiation:

Negotiation is a dynamic process that requires a strategic approach and a deep understanding of fundamental principles. Whether you're negotiating a business deal, resolving a dispute, or navigating personal relationships, mastering these principles is essential for achieving successful outcomes and building strong, collaborative partnerships. Let's explore some key principles of negotiation:

1. Willingly make concessions:

Negotiation often involves give-and-take, requiring parties to make concessions in order to reach a mutually acceptable agreement. Being willing to make concessions demonstrates flexibility and a willingness to compromise, which can help facilitate progress and build goodwill between parties. However, it's important to prioritize your core interests and objectives while being strategic about the concessions you're willing to make.

2. Do your homework:

Preparation is paramount in negotiation, and thorough research and analysis can provide a competitive advantage. Take the time to gather relevant information, understand the interests and priorities of the other party, and identify potential areas of agreement and disagreement. By arming yourself with knowledge and insight, you'll be better equipped to make informed decisions and negotiate from a position of strength.

3. Have an idea how far you want to go:

Before entering into negotiations, it's important to have a clear understanding of your goals, priorities, and boundaries. Define your objectives and establish your "walk-away" point – the point at which you're willing to walk away from the negotiation if your needs aren't being met. Having a clear sense of your bottom line allows you to negotiate with confidence and conviction while avoiding agreements that may not serve your best interests.

4. Work on building relationships:

Negotiation is not just about reaching agreements; it's also about building and maintaining relationships. Invest time and effort in building rapport and trust with the other party, as strong relationships can facilitate open communication, collaboration, and problem-solving. Approach negotiations with a mindset of mutual respect and understanding, and strive to find common ground that grows into long-term partnerships and cooperation.

5. Remain adaptable and have an open mind:

Negotiation is inherently unpredictable, and success often depends on your ability to adapt to changing circumstances and unexpected challenges. Remain flexible and open-minded throughout the negotiation process, willing to consider alternative perspectives and explore creative solutions. Embrace ambiguity and uncertainty as opportunities for growth and learning, and be prepared to pivot your approach as needed to achieve your objectives.

Strategies for Negotiation:

Negotiation is often compared to a strategic game where every move counts towards achieving your desired outcome. In this part, we'll explore negotiation strategies—practical tools and techniques designed to help you navigate discussions, resolve conflicts, and reach agreements effectively. These strategies are like keys that unlock the doors to successful negotiations, empowering you to navigate through challenges with ease and confidence. So, let's dive into the world of negotiation strategies, where simplicity meets effectiveness, and where you'll discover the secrets to mastering the art of negotiation.

1. Begin knowing where you want to end:

This strategy emphasizes the importance of setting clear objectives and defining your desired outcome before entering into negotiations. By knowing where you want to end, you can develop a strategic plan to achieve your goals and maintain focus throughout the negotiation process. Start by identifying your priorities, interests, and non-negotiables, and establish a clear vision of the ideal outcome you hope to achieve. Having a well-defined endpoint provides clarity and direction, enabling you to make informed decisions and negotiate effectively.

2. Give and take... Think about equity:

Negotiation is inherently a process of give and take, where concessions are made in exchange for concessions from the other party. This strategy emphasizes the importance of seeking equitable solutions that balance the interests and needs of both parties.

Consider the value of each concession and weigh it against what you're asking for in return. Strive to create a sense of fairness and reciprocity in the negotiation, where both parties feel that they are receiving value in exchange for what they are giving up. By approaching negotiations with a mindset of equity and fairness, you can build trust, foster cooperation, and increase the likelihood of reaching mutually beneficial agreements.

3. Let them think their deal is as good as yours:

This strategy involves framing the negotiation in a way that allows the other party to feel like they are getting a good deal, even if the terms ultimately favor your interests. By emphasizing the benefits and advantages of the proposed agreement from their perspective, you can create a sense of satisfaction and buy-in, increasing their willingness to agree to the terms. Use persuasive language and framing techniques to highlight the positive aspects of the deal for both parties, while subtly steering the negotiation towards your desired outcome. By allowing the other party to feel like they are winning, you can overcome resistance and objections more effectively, ultimately leading to a successful negotiation.

4. Don't be anxious, be confident:

Confidence is a powerful asset in negotiation, influencing how you are perceived by the other party and shaping the dynamics of the negotiation. This strategy emphasizes the importance of projecting confidence and assertiveness throughout the negotiation process. Maintain strong body language, speak with conviction, and exude self-assurance in your abilities and the value you bring to the table. Confidence instills trust and credibility, making it easier to influence the other party, overcome objections, and drive the negotiation towards your desired outcome. By cultivating a mindset of confidence and resilience, you can navigate negotiations with poise and effectiveness, increasing your chances of success.

Best Alternative to a Negotiated Agreement BATNA

BATNA, or Best Alternative to a Negotiated Agreement, is a critical concept in negotiation strategy that refers to the course of action a party will take if negotiations fail to reach a satisfactory agreement. Understanding your BATNA is essential because it provides a baseline against which to evaluate proposed agreements and informs your negotiation strategy. Here's a breakdown of each step of BATNA with examples to help illustrate its significance:

1. Identifying Alternatives:

The first step in determining your BATNA is to identify alternative options available to you if negotiations do not result in an agreement. These alternatives should be feasible, realistic, and preferably better than the proposed agreement. For example, if you're negotiating a salary raise with your employer, your alternatives might include seeking employment elsewhere, pursuing additional education or certifications to enhance your qualifications, or starting your own business.

2. Evaluating Alternatives:

Once you've identified potential alternatives, evaluate each one based on its feasibility, desirability, and potential outcomes. Consider factors such as financial implications, career advancement opportunities, work-life balance, and personal values. Compare the potential benefits and drawbacks of each alternative to assess their relative strengths and weaknesses. For instance, if you're considering seeking employment elsewhere as an alternative to negotiating a salary raise, evaluate factors such as job market conditions, potential salary increases, job satisfaction, and career growth prospects at alternative employers.

3. Determining BATNA:

Based on your evaluation of alternatives, determine which alternative represents your Best Alternative to a Negotiated Agreement (BATNA). Your BATNA is the option that you would pursue if negotiations fail to result in a satisfactory agreement. It should be the most attractive alternative available to you, providing a viable fallback position that meets your needs and objectives. For example, if you determine that receiving a job offer from a competing company with a higher salary and better benefits package is your most attractive alternative, then that becomes your BATNA in negotiations with your current employer for a salary raise.

Significance in Negotiation Strategy:

Understanding your BATNA is crucial because it serves as a reference point for assessing the value of potential agreements and guiding your negotiation strategy. If the proposed agreement is better than your BATNA, it may be advantageous to accept the offer. However, if the proposed agreement is inferior to your BATNA, it may be in your best interest to walk away from the negotiation and pursue your BATNA instead. By knowing your BATNA, you can negotiate from a position of strength, confidently rejecting offers that fall short of your alternative options and potentially securing more favorable outcomes. Additionally, having a strong BATNA increases your bargaining power and leverage in negotiations, as the other party is aware that you have viable alternatives and are not dependent solely on reaching an agreement with them. Overall, incorporating BATNA analysis into your negotiation strategy enables you to make informed decisions, maximize value, and achieve your objectives more effectively.

Negotiating for Success

Negotiating salary increases or promotions in the workplace can be a daunting task, but with careful preparation and strategic approach, it can also be an opportunity to advocate for your worth and advance your career. In this section, we'll explore specific techniques for negotiating salary increases or promotions, equipping you with the knowledge and skills needed to navigate these discussions with confidence and success.

- **Research the market for competitive salaries in that particular field:**

Before entering into negotiations, it's essential to gather information about the prevailing market rates for salaries in your industry and geographic location. Research online resources, industry reports, and salary surveys to gain insights into what professionals with similar skills and experience are earning. Armed with this information, you can make a compelling case for why you deserve a salary increase or promotion based on industry standards and market trends.

For example, suppose you're a software engineer seeking a salary increase. You research salary data for software engineers with comparable skills and experience in your city and discover that the average salary is higher than what you're currently earning. Armed with this information, you can confidently advocate for a salary increase that aligns with market rates and reflects your value to the company.

- **Be prepared to state your value:**

During negotiations, it's crucial to articulate the value you bring to the organization and how your contributions have positively impacted its success. Highlight your accomplishments, skills, and qualifications that make you uniquely qualified for a salary increase or promotion. Provide concrete examples of projects you've led, results you've achieved, and ways you've added value to the company.

For instance, if you're seeking a promotion to a managerial role, you can discuss how you've successfully managed cross-functional teams, improved operational efficiency, and contributed to revenue growth. By demonstrating your value and impact, you strengthen your position and justify your request for a salary increase or promotion.

- **Indicate how the company or institution has benefited from your blood, sweat, and tears:**

Emphasize the specific ways in which your contributions have contributed to the company's success and bottom line. Quantify your achievements whenever possible, such as increased sales revenue, cost savings, or improvements in productivity. By highlighting the tangible benefits of your efforts, you underscore your value to the organization and strengthen your case for a salary increase or promotion.

For example, if you're a marketing manager, you can discuss how your innovative marketing campaigns have generated leads, increased brand visibility, and contributed to revenue growth. By showcasing the direct impact of your work on the company's success, you demonstrate your worth and justify your request for a salary increase or promotion.

- **Share short and long-term growth strategies that will benefit the company or institution:**

Demonstrate your commitment to the company's long-term success by outlining your vision and strategies for driving growth and innovation. Discuss your ideas for expanding market reach, improving operational efficiency, or developing new products or services. By presenting proactive solutions and initiatives, you position yourself as a strategic thinker and valuable asset to the organization, deserving of a salary increase or promotion.

For instance, if you're a sales manager, you can propose strategies for penetrating new markets, optimizing sales processes, and enhancing customer engagement to drive revenue growth. By showcasing your strategic thinking and vision for the company's future, you reinforce your value proposition and justify your request for a salary increase or promotion.

- **Indicate ways the company or institution can build wealth:**

Highlight opportunities for the company to increase profitability, reduce costs, or gain a competitive edge in the market. Discuss your ideas for revenue generation, cost-saving initiatives, or strategic partnerships that can enhance the company's financial performance and create value for stakeholders. By demonstrating your understanding of the company's business objectives and offering innovative solutions, you position yourself as a strategic partner and invaluable asset to the organization.

For example, if you're a finance manager, you can propose cost-saving measures, investment opportunities, or financial strategies to optimize cash flow and maximize profitability. By showcasing your financial acumen and ability to drive business growth, you underscore your value to the company and justify your request for a salary increase or promotion.

Personal Negotiation Stories

For a recent birthday party, I hired an entertainer at a set price. However, during our negotiations, I proposed an enticing opportunity for the entertainer to perform at three additional venues. While I offered a lower price—25% less than the original fee—the entertainer saw the potential for significant benefits beyond immediate financial gain. By accepting the reduced rate, the entertainer gained exposure to new audiences and opportunities to showcase their talents. This not only provided immediate income but also served as a valuable investment in building credibility and expanding their client base. Ultimately, both parties benefited from the negotiation: I received quality entertainment at a discounted rate, while the entertainer secured multiple bookings and enhanced their reputation in the industry.

In another negotiation scenario, I approached a catering company with an opportunity to serve a school at a competitive rate of $25 per head. Recognizing the potential for additional business, I secured commitments from four other schools to hire the catering company at the same price. In exchange for bringing in this extra business, the catering company agreed to lower their price to $20 per head for the initial school event. This mutually beneficial arrangement not only allowed the catering company to capitalize on multiple opportunities for revenue but also solidified my role as a valuable intermediary. As a result, two out of the four schools decided to establish ongoing contracts with the catering company, further solidifying the success of the negotiation.

In this chapter, we've explored the art of negotiation, from understanding key principles and strategies to applying them in real-life scenarios. Through personal anecdotes and case studies, we've witnessed the transformative power of negotiation in achieving favorable outcomes and building mutually beneficial relationships. Whether negotiating salary increases, securing business contracts, or resolving conflicts, the principles of negotiation serve as invaluable tools for navigating life's challenges with confidence and effectiveness.

As we conclude this chapter, it's clear that negotiation is a skill that transcends boundaries and empowers individuals to advocate for their interests and achieve their goals. In the next chapter, we'll shift our focus to the importance of effective communication, exploring strategies for building rapport, resolving conflicts, and fostering understanding in diverse settings.

CHAPTER 3

COMMUNICATE WITH IMPACT

Effective communication is the foundation of personal and professional success, allowing us to convey our thoughts, feelings, and ideas with clarity and confidence. In this chapter, we'll explore the art of communicating with impact, focusing on both verbal and nonverbal aspects of communication. From mastering the power of words to harnessing the subtleties of body language, we'll uncover practical strategies for building rapport, resolving conflicts, and develop understanding in diverse settings.

Effective communication encompasses both verbal and nonverbal elements. Verbal communication refers to the use of words to convey messages, express thoughts, and engage in dialogue. It encompasses spoken language, tone of voice, and choice of words, all of which play a crucial role in shaping the effectiveness of communication.

When communicating verbally, it's important to speak clearly, concisely, and with confidence. Pay attention to your tone of voice, volume, and pacing to convey sincerity and authority. For example, imagine you're giving a presentation at work. By speaking clearly and confidently, using a conversational tone, and varying your pitch and volume to emphasize key points, you can capture the audience's attention and convey your message with impact.

Nonverbal communication, on the other hand, refers to the use of body language, facial expressions, gestures, and other nonverbal cues to convey meaning and emotions. It often speaks louder than words and can significantly influence how a message is perceived. Nonverbal cues such as eye contact, facial expressions, posture, and hand gestures can convey confidence, sincerity, and empathy, enhancing the impact of communication.

For instance, during a job interview, maintaining eye contact, sitting up straight, and using open gestures can project confidence and professionalism, leaving a positive impression on the interviewer.

The most effective communication occurs when verbal and nonverbal cues align to reinforce the intended message. By paying attention to both aspects of communication, you can enhance your ability to connect with others, build rapport, and convey your message with clarity and impact. Practice active listening, empathetic understanding, and genuine engagement to create meaningful connections and grow mutual understanding.

In this chapter, we are going to explore the importance of communicating with impact, focusing on both verbal and nonverbal aspects of communication. By mastering the art of verbal communication and harnessing the power of nonverbal cues, you can enhance your ability to convey messages effectively, build strong relationships, and achieve your personal and professional goals. Join us as we delve deeper into the principles of effective communication, exploring strategies for resolving conflicts, navigating diversity, and developing empathy in the next section.

Importance of Effective Communication

Effective communication is the lifeblood of both personal and professional success, serving as the bridge that connects individuals, fosters understanding, and drives meaningful interactions. In personal life, effective communication nurtures relationships, builds trust, and enhances intimacy. It enables individuals to express their thoughts, feelings, and desires authentically, leading to deeper connections and stronger bonds with loved ones. In the professional realm, effective communication is equally vital, facilitating collaboration, and driving innovation. It empowers individuals to articulate their ideas, influence others, and navigate complex workplace dynamics with confidence and clarity. Whether in personal or professional contexts, mastering the art of communication empowers individuals to navigate life's challenges, build meaningful connections, and achieve their goals with grace and effectiveness. Let's explore how effective communication contributes to both personal and professional success through the following points:

1. Team building:

Effective communication is essential for building strong and cohesive teams. By nurturing open dialogue, active listening, and mutual respect, team members can collaborate more effectively, share ideas, and work towards common goals. Clear communication helps to minimize misunderstandings and conflicts, promoting a positive team culture where trust and camaraderie thrive. As a result, teams can achieve higher levels of productivity, creativity, and success.

2. Makes you an innovator, creator, humanist:

Effective communication empowers individuals to express their ideas, share insights, and inspire others. By communicating effectively, you can articulate your vision, influence others, and drive innovation and creativity. Whether you're leading a project, presenting a proposal, or collaborating with colleagues, the ability to communicate persuasively and compellingly can differentiate you as an innovator, creator, and humanist who inspires positive change and progress.

3. Develops skills you already have:

Effective communication enhances and develops existing skills, enabling individuals to become more proficient in their roles and more adaptable to changing circumstances. Through communication, individuals can refine their listening skills, articulate their thoughts more clearly, and navigate complex situations with confidence and poise. By continually honing their communication skills, individuals can unlock their full potential and achieve greater success in both personal and professional endeavors.

4. Leads to employee satisfaction and engagement:

Effective communication contributes to a positive work environment where employees feel valued, respected, and engaged. When leaders communicate openly and transparently, employees feel more informed and connected to the organization's mission and goals. This sense of alignment and purpose leads to higher levels of job satisfaction, morale, and motivation. Moreover, effective communication encourages feedback and dialogue, allowing employees to voice their concerns, contribute ideas, and actively participate in decision-making processes, which further enhances their sense of ownership and engagement.

Communication in workplace and personal life:

Communication is the basis of every relationship, shaping the way we connect, understand, and relate to one another. Whether in the workplace or in personal life, effective communication is essential for building trust, growing collaboration, and nurturing meaningful connections. However, when communication falters, it can have far-reaching consequences, impacting relationships in profound ways. Let's explore how communication impacts relationships both within the workplace and in personal life through the following points:

1. If not clear, communication can change the meaning of a message or statement in both personal and workplace contexts. Misinterpretations or misunderstandings can arise when communication lacks clarity or precision, leading to confusion, conflict, and frustration. In personal relationships, a miscommunication can cause hurt feelings or resentment, while in the workplace, it can result in errors, delays, and decreased productivity.

2. In both personal and professional settings, people may second-guess you if your communication is unclear or ambiguous. Doubt or uncertainty about the intended message can erode trust and confidence, leading others to question your credibility or intentions. Clear and transparent communication is essential for

building trust and maintaining strong relationships based on mutual respect and understanding.

3. Communication that lacks clarity or specificity can appear to be a game of semantics, where the true meaning of the message becomes obscured by vague language or ambiguous statements. In the workplace, this can lead to confusion about roles, responsibilities, and expectations, undermining team cohesion and productivity. Similarly, in personal relationships, ambiguous communication can create tension or frustration, as individuals struggle to discern the true intentions behind the words.

4. In the workplace, communication plays a critical role in shaping a person's credibility and respect. Effective communicators are viewed as trustworthy, competent, and reliable, inspiring confidence and respect from colleagues and supervisors alike. Conversely, poor communication skills can undermine a person's credibility, leading to misunderstandings, conflicts, and diminished professional reputation.

5. Similarly, in personal life, communication is the foundation of trust and intimacy. When communication is clear, honest, and open, it develops deeper connections and strengthens bonds between individuals. However, when communication breaks down or is characterized by dishonesty or avoidance, trust can be eroded, leading to resentment, conflict, and ultimately, relationship breakdown.

Developing Communication Skills:

Developing communication skills may seem daunting at first, but it's actually more straightforward than you might think. Just like any other skill, improving communication is about practice and persistence. You don't need to reinvent the wheel or master complex techniques overnight. Instead, focus on making small, consistent improvements over time. Engage in conversations, actively listen to others, and pay attention to your own speaking habits. Reflect on your interactions and consider areas where you can make adjustments. Remember, communication is a skill that can be developed and refined with practice. So, don't be afraid to jump in and start follow the next section to help yourself communicate effectively.

Practical exercises and tips to improve verbal communication skills:

Improving verbal communication skills doesn't always require formal training or elaborate exercises. Instead, it often comes down to small, intentional actions that can be integrated into everyday interactions. Here are some practical exercises and activities individuals can do to enhance their verbal communication skills:

1. Become a better listener:

Becoming a better listener involves more than just hearing what someone else is saying. It requires active engagement and attention to the speaker's words, tone, and body language. To improve your listening skills, practice giving your full attention to the speaker, maintaining eye contact, and nodding or using other nonverbal cues to show you're engaged. Avoid distractions and resist the urge to interrupt or formulate your response while the speaker is talking. Instead, focus on understanding the speaker's message and empathizing with their perspective.

2. Be quick to listen and slow to speak:

This principle, often attributed to the book of James in the Bible, emphasizes the importance of prioritizing listening over speaking in communication. By being quick to listen, you demonstrate respect for the speaker and a willingness to understand their perspective before expressing your own. Avoid rushing to respond or interjecting your thoughts before the speaker has finished conveying their message. Instead, take the time to fully comprehend what the speaker is saying before formulating your response.

3. Be an active listener:

Active listening involves more than just hearing the words spoken by the speaker. It requires genuine engagement, empathy, and a desire to understand the speaker's message. To be an active listener, approach conversations with an open mind and a genuine curiosity about the speaker's perspective. Avoid listening solely to respond or waiting for your turn to speak. Instead, focus on fully understanding the speaker's message, asking clarifying questions when needed, and providing feedback to show you're engaged and attentive.

4. Ask open-ended questions:

Open-ended questions are questions that require more than a simple yes or no answer. They invite the speaker to share their thoughts, feelings, and experiences more fully, fostering deeper conversation and rapport. To improve your verbal communication skills, practice asking open-ended questions that encourage the speaker to elaborate on their ideas or provide additional information. For example, instead of asking, "Did you enjoy the presentation?" you could ask, "What did you find most interesting about the presentation?"

5. Ask for clarification when needed:

Communication can sometimes be ambiguous or unclear, leading to misunderstandings or confusion. To prevent miscommunication, don't hesitate to ask for clarification if you're unsure about something the speaker said. Asking for clarification demonstrates active listening and a genuine desire to understand the speaker's message more fully. It also helps to ensure that both parties are on the same page and prevents misunderstandings from escalating.

Becoming Mindful of Nonverbal Communication

Nonverbal communication encompasses all forms of communication that do not involve spoken or written words. It includes gestures, facial expressions, body language, tone of voice, and other subtle cues that convey meaning and emotions in interpersonal interactions. While verbal communication provides the content of the message, nonverbal cues often provide context, emphasis, and emotional cues that shape how the message is interpreted. In fact, research suggests that nonverbal communication can convey up to 93% of the total message in face-to-face communication, highlighting its significant impact on understanding and interpretation.

Nonverbal communication plays a crucial role in interpersonal communication, influencing how messages are perceived, understood, and interpreted. It helps individuals express emotions, convey attitudes, and establish rapport with others. For example, a warm smile and a friendly handshake can communicate openness and trust, while crossed arms and a furrowed brow may indicate defensiveness or discomfort. Additionally, nonverbal cues provide valuable feedback to speakers, helping them gauge the effectiveness of their message and adjust their communication accordingly.

Now, let's explore how individuals can become more mindful of their nonverbal communication cues, such as body language and tone of voice:

1. Make sure speech ties in with behaviors:

When communicating, it's essential to ensure that your verbal message aligns with your nonverbal cues. Your body language, facial expressions, and tone of voice should complement and reinforce the message you're conveying verbally. For example, if you're expressing enthusiasm about a project, your body language should reflect that enthusiasm through gestures, posture, and facial expressions. Incongruence between verbal and nonverbal cues can lead to confusion or mistrust, as listeners may perceive inconsistency or insincerity in your communication.

2. Use appropriate gestures and signals:

Gestures can enhance communication by adding emphasis, clarity, and visual interest to your message. However, it's essential to use gestures appropriately and in moderation. Be mindful of cultural differences and context when using gestures, as what may be considered acceptable in one culture could be perceived differently in another. Avoid overly exaggerated or distracting gestures that may detract from your message or convey unintended meanings. Instead, use gestures sparingly to complement and reinforce your verbal message, adding emphasis or illustrating key points.

3. Regulate voice tone:

Your tone of voice can significantly influence how your message is received and interpreted by others. Practice modulating your tone to match the content and emotional context of your message. For example, when delivering good news or expressing appreciation, use a warm and positive tone to convey sincerity and enthusiasm. Conversely, when discussing sensitive topics or delivering constructive feedback, adopt a calm and empathetic tone to convey empathy and understanding. Be mindful of your volume, pitch, and intonation, as these elements can also convey meaning and emotional nuances in communication.

4. Ask open-ended questions:

Encourage deeper conversation and engagement by asking open-ended questions that invite others to share their thoughts, feelings, and experiences. Open-ended questions prompt individuals to provide more detailed and substantive responses, encouraging meaningful dialogue and connection. For example, instead of asking a yes/no question like, "Did you enjoy the presentation?" you could ask an open-ended question like, "What aspects of the presentation did you find most interesting or insightful?" This encourages the speaker to elaborate on their thoughts and provides an opportunity for deeper discussion.

5. Know the context:

Consider the situational context and cultural norms when interpreting nonverbal cues and adjusting your own communication style. Different contexts may require different nonverbal cues, so it's essential to adapt your behavior accordingly to ensure effective communication. For example, in a formal business meeting, you may adopt a more professional demeanor with reserved body language and tone of voice. In contrast, in a casual social setting, you may feel more relaxed and expressive with your gestures and speech. By understanding the context and cultural norms, you can navigate interpersonal interactions more effectively and build stronger connections with others.

Personal Communication Challenges:

During a business meeting, I encountered a situation where effective communication played a crucial role in overcoming a significant obstacle. As the meeting progressed, I noticed that the Asian businesspeople present were avoiding eye contact, which struck me as unusual. Understanding that in their culture, avoiding direct eye contact is a sign of respect and politeness, especially when interacting with authority figures or elders, I realized the cultural difference at play. In contrast, in American culture, eye contact is often seen as a sign of respect across all age groups. Recognizing the potential for misunderstanding, I knew that clear communication was essential to address the situation.

After the meeting, I took the initiative to communicate with the group, acknowledging the cultural differences and providing context to ensure mutual understanding. I explained that the Asian individuals' behavior was a demonstration of respect in their culture and not a lack of engagement or interest. By offering this explanation, I helped bridge the gap in understanding between the two cultural perspectives, having mutual respect and appreciation. This experience highlighted the importance of effective communication in navigating cultural differences and building strong relationships in a diverse and globalized world.

In conclusion, effective communication is not just a skill—it's a powerful tool that shapes our interactions, relationships, and ultimately, our success in both personal and professional realms. Throughout this chapter, we've explored the intricacies of communication, from verbal and nonverbal cues to the importance of cultural awareness and empathy. We've learned that by honing our communication skills, we can build trust, foster understanding, and navigate even the most challenging situations with grace and confidence.

As we move forward, let's remember that communication is not a one-size-fits-all endeavor. It requires active listening, adaptability, and a willingness to engage with others authentically. By continuing to cultivate our communication skills and embracing the diversity of perspectives and experiences around us, we can create connections that transcend boundaries and lead to greater collaboration, innovation, and mutual respect.

So, let's commit to being mindful communicators, recognizing the power of our words and actions to shape the world around us. Together, let's strive to communicate with empathy, integrity, and intentionality, knowing that our ability to connect with others is the cornerstone of our personal and professional success.

CHAPTER 4

CULTIVATING POSITIVE MINDSETS

In the journey of life, our mindset plays a profound role in shaping our experiences and outcomes. A positive mindset is not just about being optimistic or seeing the world through rose-colored glasses; it's about cultivating a mindset that empowers us to navigate challenges, embrace opportunities, and thrive in both personal and professional spheres.

Cultivating a positive mindset begins with recognizing the power of our thoughts and attitudes. It's about choosing to focus on the possibilities rather than the limitations, the solutions rather than the problems. In our personal lives, a positive mindset enables us to approach relationships, setbacks, and everyday challenges with resilience, optimism, and grace. It allows us to bounce back from adversity, find joy in the little moments, and cultivate deeper connections with ourselves and others.

In the professional realm, a positive mindset is equally essential. It fuels creativity, innovation, and problem-solving, empowering us to adapt to change, take calculated risks, and pursue our goals with confidence. A positive mindset fosters a culture of collaboration, trust, and growth within teams and organizations, driving productivity, engagement, and success.

But how do we cultivate a positive mindset amidst life's inevitable ups and downs? It begins with self-awareness and mindfulness—being conscious of our thoughts, emotions, and reactions. By practicing gratitude, focusing on our strengths, and reframing negative thoughts, we can train our minds to see the good even in challenging situations. Surrounding ourselves with positive influences, seeking support when needed, and prioritizing self-care also play crucial roles in nurturing a positive mindset.

In our personal lives, cultivating a positive mindset is essential for our overall well-being and happiness. It influences how we perceive ourselves, relate to others, and navigate the various challenges and joys that life brings. Here's why cultivating a positive mindset is crucial in personal life:

Cultivating a positive mindset enhances resilience, helping us bounce back from setbacks with hope and perseverance. It fosters healthier relationships by promoting empathy, understanding, and appreciation with family, friends, and loved ones. Positivity promotes emotional well-being by managing stress, anxiety, and depression through reframing negative thoughts and self-care activities.

A positive mindset boosts self-esteem and confidence, empowering us to pursue our passions and embrace new opportunities for growth and fulfillment. It encourages a solution-oriented approach to problem-solving, fostering creativity and learning from setbacks. Cultivating positivity also nurtures gratitude, allowing us to appreciate life's blessings and find joy in simple pleasures, leading to greater overall happiness and fulfillment in our daily lives.

Ultimately, cultivating a positive mindset is not a destination but a journey—a daily practice of choosing hope over despair, gratitude over resentment, and growth over stagnation. It's about embracing the inherent potential within ourselves and the world around us, knowing that our mindset has the power to shape our reality and create a life filled with purpose, resilience, and joy.

The Impact of Maintaining a Positive Mindset on Resilience and Success

Maintaining a positive mindset is akin to nurturing a mental garden where the seeds of optimism and hope flourish, even amidst the harshest of conditions. In our journey through life, this mindset serves as a guiding light, illuminating the path to resilience and success. Let's delve into how maintaining a positive mindset impacts resilience and success:

1. Positive Mindset Equals Positive Actions:

In the face of challenges, maintaining a positive mindset serves as your catalyst for positive actions. With a positive outlook, you're more inclined to approach obstacles with determination, resourcefulness, and a can-do attitude. Instead of succumbing to despair or giving in to negativity, you channel your energy into productive endeavors, seeking solutions and opportunities for growth.

2. Positive Thinking Unlocks Challenges and Creates Opportunities:

Positivity isn't merely a state of mind; it's a potent force that unlocks doors and windows of opportunity, even in the toughest times. When you maintain a positive mindset, you view challenges as chances for growth and transformation. Setbacks become stepping stones to success, as you reframe obstacles as valuable learning experiences that propel you forward on your journey.

3. Encourages the Development of New Skills:

When you maintain a positive mindset, you're encouraged to step out of your comfort zone and embrace new challenges. In this process, you cultivate resilience by developing new skills, expanding your capabilities, and honing your strengths. Each hurdle you overcome leaves you stronger, more adaptable, and better equipped to navigate future obstacles.

4. Keeps Focus:

Amidst life's distractions and uncertainties, your positive mindset serves as a compass, guiding you toward your goals and aspirations. It helps you maintain focus amidst chaos, stay committed to your vision, and persevere through setbacks. By keeping your eyes on the prize and your mind attuned to possibilities, you forge ahead with confidence and determination.

5. Open Ended Tunnel:

Finally, maintaining a positive mindset opens the door to an endless tunnel of possibilities. It fosters an attitude of optimism and hope, even in the darkest of times. Instead of seeing limitations, you with a positive outlook see boundless potential and endless horizons. This open-ended tunnel of possibilities fuels your resilience and propels you toward success, no matter the challenges you may face.

Strategies for Cultivating Positivity:

Shifting negative thought patterns is a journey toward empowering yourself and fostering a more positive mindset. Here are some practical techniques that can help you in this transformative process:

1. Be Optimistic, Not Pessimistic:

Embrace a mindset that looks for the silver lining in every situation. Instead of dwelling on what could go wrong, focus on what could go right. Train your mind to see challenges as opportunities for growth and learning.

2. Always Focus on the End Goal:

Keep your eyes on the prize and concentrate on what you're striving to achieve. Visualize yourself succeeding and let that vision guide your actions and decisions. Remind yourself of the bigger picture whenever negative thoughts creep in.

3. Practice Self-Affirmations:

Use positive affirmations to challenge and overcome self-doubt. Repeat phrases such as "I am capable," "I am worthy," and "I am enough" to reaffirm your self-worth and potential. Believe in yourself and your abilities.

4. Read and Research for Self-Esteem Building:

Invest in personal development by reading books, articles, and resources that inspire and motivate you. Surround yourself with material that uplifts and empowers you. Build your self-esteem through knowledge and preparation, knowing that readiness meets opportunity.

5. Associate with Positive People:

Surround yourself with individuals who radiate positivity and support your growth. Positive energy is contagious, and being around optimistic people can uplift your spirits and reinforce your own positive outlook. Remember, birds of a feather flock together.

6. Visualize Success:

Take time to visualize yourself achieving your goals and dreams. Close your eyes and imagine yourself succeeding, feeling the emotions of accomplishment and fulfillment. Visualization can help instill confidence and belief in yourself.

Specific Exercises for Developing a Positive Mindset:

Embarking on the journey of developing a positive mindset is an investment in your overall well-being and happiness. Here are some specific exercises and practices that can help foster a positive mindset and cultivate a more optimistic outlook on life:

1. Encourage Yourself:

Start each day with words of encouragement and self-affirmation. Speak to yourself kindly and motivate yourself with positive affirmations. Remind yourself of your strengths, capabilities, and past successes. By nurturing a supportive inner dialogue, you can boost your confidence and resilience.

2. Practice Gratitude:

Cultivate an attitude of gratitude by reflecting on the things you're thankful for each day. Keep a gratitude journal and write down three things you're grateful for every morning or evening. Focusing on the positive aspects of your life can shift your perspective and foster feelings of contentment and joy.

3. Engage in Specific Self-Affirmations:

Create personalized self-affirmations that resonate with you and address areas where you seek growth or improvement. For example, if you struggle with self-confidence, affirmations like "I am confident in my abilities" or "I believe in myself and my potential" can be empowering. Repeat these affirmations regularly to reinforce positive beliefs about yourself.

4. Take Care of Yourself:

Prioritize self-care practices that nourish your mind, body, and soul. Ensure you're getting enough rest, staying hydrated, eating a balanced diet, and engaging in regular exercise. Physical well-being is closely linked to mental health, and taking care of yourself holistically can boost your mood and energy levels.

5. Feed Your Mind with Positive Content:

Surround yourself with uplifting and inspiring content that feeds your mind with positivity. Listen to motivational podcasts, read uplifting books and articles, and follow social media accounts that promote positivity and personal growth. Fill your mind with empowering messages and ideas that reinforce your positive mindset.

Overcoming Adversity:

Throughout history, individuals from all walks of life have faced adversity with resilience and optimism, using the power of positive thinking to overcome seemingly insurmountable obstacles. Here are some of my inspiring personal stories of individuals who defied the odds through their unwavering belief in themselves and the strength of positive thinking:

Bernard H. Jones, Sr., my father, despite a very poor upbringing in a single-parent household reliant on welfare, refused to let his circumstances define his future. With the guidance and encouragement of his mother and mentors like the late Rev. Cornell Talley, he embraced the power of positive thinking and self-belief. Despite facing numerous challenges, including his mother's health struggles and his own battle with tuberculosis that ended his football career, my father remained steadfast in his determination to succeed.

Overcoming Health Challenges:

My father's journey was fraught with adversity, including his mother's health challenges and his own battle with tuberculosis, which left him hospitalized for six months. However, through the power of positive thinking instilled in him by his mother and mentors, my father persevered. He emerged from these trials with a renewed sense of purpose and resilience, ready to tackle whatever challenges lay ahead.

Community Transformation:

Inspired by his own experiences, my father dedicated his life to uplifting others and transforming his community. He founded several programs and initiatives aimed at empowering African American youth and fostering positive change, including the Pittsburgh African American Development, UMP Investments, Retism, Urban Youth Action, and the POISE Foundation. Through these endeavors, my father was able to touch the lives of thousands, leaving a lasting legacy of hope, opportunity, and empowerment.

In closing, the stories shared here highlight the transformative power of cultivating positivity in overcoming life's challenges and achieving extraordinary accomplishments. As we reflect on these journeys, let us be inspired to nurture a positive mindset in our own lives, knowing that optimism and self-belief can light the path to resilience and success. In the next chapter, we will delve into the importance of building resilience in the face of adversity, exploring strategies to overcome obstacles with strength and perseverance.

CHAPTER 5

BUILDING RESILIENCE IN ADVERSITY

Life is a journey filled with twists and turns, highs and lows, triumphs and trials. Along the way, we encounter challenges that test our resolve, shake our confidence, and push us to our limits. In the face of adversity, the ability to bounce back and thrive is paramount. This is where resilience comes into play.

Resilience is more than just bouncing back from setbacks; it's about bouncing forward. It's the capacity to adapt, grow, and thrive in the face of adversity. Resilient individuals possess inner strength, perseverance, and the ability to overcome obstacles with grace and determination.

In this chapter, we will embark on a journey to explore the concept of resilience in depth. We'll uncover its significance in navigating life's challenges and learn practical strategies for building resilience. From cultivating a positive mindset to developing coping skills, we'll delve into the key components of resilience and discover how to harness its power to overcome adversity and thrive in the face of uncertainty.

Understanding Resilience:

In the African American community, resilience has been a cornerstone of survival and progress throughout history. From enduring the horrors of slavery to facing systemic injustices, African Americans have demonstrated remarkable resilience in the face of adversity. Resilience is the ability to bounce back and thrive despite facing challenges and setbacks. It's about finding strength in the midst of struggle and emerging stronger on the other side.

Resilience is especially important in overcoming obstacles and setbacks because it provides the opportunity to recover quickly from difficulties. Life is filled with many trials and tribulations, but resilience empowers you to navigate these challenges with courage and grace. Here's why resilience is crucial:

Helps to Get Away from Depression and Anxiety: Resilience acts as a protective factor against mental health issues such as depression and anxiety. By cultivating resilience, you build the inner strength and coping mechanisms needed to overcome adversity and maintain emotional well-being.

1. Helps with Trauma:

Resilience enables individuals to process and heal from traumatic experiences. Instead of being overwhelmed by trauma, resilient individuals are better equipped to cope with the aftermath and move forward with their lives.

2. Helps with Mental Health Situations:

Resilience plays a vital role in promoting mental health and well-being. It equips individuals with the skills and mindset needed to navigate life's challenges and maintain a positive outlook, even in the face of adversity.

3. Gives Hope:

Resilience instills hope and optimism for the future. It reminds us that setbacks are temporary and that we have the strength and resilience to overcome them. By cultivating resilience, individuals can find hope even in the darkest of times.

4. Encourages Unity:

Resilience fosters a sense of unity and community support. When individuals come together to support one another through difficult times, it strengthens bonds and creates a sense of solidarity that helps everyone involved to overcome adversity.

5. Dealing with Adversity:

Resilience equips individuals with the skills and mindset needed to effectively deal with adversity. Instead of being overwhelmed by challenges, resilient individuals are able to face them head-on, adapt to changing circumstances, and emerge stronger on the other side.

Role of Resilience in Contributing Personal Growth and Development:

In your journey of personal growth and development, resilience plays a crucial role in shaping your mindset and approach to life. Here's how resilience contributes to your personal growth:

1. More Aware of Higher Spiritual Power:

Cultivating resilience often leads to a deeper awareness of a higher spiritual power at work in your life. As you face challenges and setbacks, you may find strength and solace in faith, spirituality, or a sense of purpose beyond yourself. This awareness can provide comfort and guidance, helping you navigate difficult times with grace and resilience.

2. Embracing Diversity in Approaches:

Resilience teaches you that there's more than one way to approach a problem or situation. Rather than feeling restricted by narrow-minded thinking, resilient individuals are open to exploring different perspectives and solutions. This flexibility and openness to diversity in approaches allow for creative problem-solving and personal growth.

3. Steering Away from Worry:

Resilience empowers you to navigate uncertainty and adversity without succumbing to worry or anxiety. Instead of dwelling on worst-case scenarios, resilient individuals focus on taking proactive steps to address challenges and overcome obstacles. This mindset shift from worry to action fosters inner peace and mental well-being, enabling you to approach life's challenges with confidence and resilience.

4. Enhanced Self-Control and Temperance:

Building resilience involves developing self-control and temperance in the face of adversity. Rather than reacting impulsively or becoming overwhelmed by emotions, resilient individuals maintain composure and clarity of thought. This self-control allows for better decision-making and problem-solving, contributing to personal growth and development.

5. Fostering Integrity:

Resilience is closely linked to integrity, as it involves staying true to your values and principles even in the face of adversity. Resilient individuals uphold their integrity by remaining steadfast in their beliefs and ethical standards, even when confronted with challenges or temptations. This commitment to integrity builds trust, credibility, and personal character, contributing to overall growth and development.

Strategies for Building Resilience:

Developing resilience is a journey that involves cultivating inner strength, perseverance, and the ability to navigate life's challenges with grace and determination. Here are some practical techniques for developing resilience:

1. Believe in Yourself and Your Abilities:

One of the first steps in building resilience is to believe in yourself and your abilities. Cultivate a mindset of self-confidence and self-efficacy, recognizing that you have the power to overcome obstacles and achieve your goals. By embracing a positive self-image and trusting in your capabilities, you lay the foundation for resilience in the face of adversity.

2. Recognize that Problems are Temporary:

Resilient individuals understand that problems and setbacks are temporary and that they have the capacity to overcome them. Instead of becoming overwhelmed by challenges, they maintain perspective and focus on finding solutions. By viewing obstacles as temporary hurdles rather than insurmountable barriers, you can approach them with resilience and determination.

3. Develop Stamina:

Resilience requires stamina – both physical and mental. Building resilience involves developing the endurance to persevere through difficult times, even when faced with fatigue or adversity. Engage in activities that promote physical health and well-being, such as regular exercise, healthy eating, and adequate rest. Additionally, cultivate mental stamina through practices such as mindfulness, meditation, and stress management techniques.

4. Elevate Your Mind:

Resilience begins in the mind, and cultivating a positive and resilient mindset is essential for building resilience. Elevate your mind by focusing on positive thoughts, practicing gratitude, and reframing negative experiences into opportunities for growth. Cultivate optimism and resilience by surrounding yourself with positive influences, seeking out inspirational resources, and nurturing a sense of hope and possibility.

Learning from Setbacks:

Amidst the relentless waves of financial hardship crashing down upon her, a friend found herself facing an insurmountable debt totaling $90,000 owed in loans to Bank of America, Truist, and Apple Federal Credit Union. Adding to the weight of her burdens, she also found herself behind on tax payments. However, rather than succumb to despair, she chose to confront her challenges head-on. Seeking guidance from a tax advisor (CPA) and a financial coach, she embarked on a journey to tackle her debt and regain control of her financial future.

With unwavering determination and a commitment to change, she devised a plan to pay off her debt within seven years. Through diligent budgeting, strategic financial planning, and savvy utilization of tax loopholes and forgiveness programs, she surpassed her own expectations. What was initially projected to be a seven-year journey was completed in just three years. Her resilience in the face of adversity not only enabled her to overcome her financial struggles but also taught her invaluable lessons about resourcefulness, perseverance, and the power of resilience. Through her experience, she discovered that failure and adversity are not roadblocks but opportunities for growth and transformation. She emerged from the depths of hardship stronger, wiser, and more resilient than ever before.

As we conclude this chapter on resilience, let us reflect on the profound lessons learned from stories of triumph over adversity. In the words of Maya Angelou, "You may encounter many defeats, but you must not be defeated. In fact, it may be necessary to encounter the defeats, so you can know who you are, what you can rise from, how you can still come out of it." These stories remind us that resilience is not just about bouncing back; it's about bouncing forward with newfound strength, wisdom, and resilience.

As you continue your journey, remember that resilience is a skill that can be cultivated and strengthened through perseverance, courage, and a positive mindset. Embrace life's challenges as opportunities for growth and transformation, knowing that with resilience, you have the power to overcome any obstacle that comes your way.

CHAPTER 6

NURTURING SOCIAL AND EMOTIONAL INTELLIGENCE

Have you ever found yourself in a situation where understanding and managing your emotions were crucial for a successful outcome? Picture this: you're in a heated discussion with a colleague about a project deadline. Tensions are rising, and both of you are on edge. In that moment, your ability to stay calm, empathize with your colleague's perspective, and communicate effectively can make all the difference between a constructive resolution and escalating conflict.

These scenarios are part of our everyday lives, whether in the workplace, within our families, or in social settings. They highlight the importance of social and emotional intelligence—the ability to recognize, understand, and manage emotions, both in ourselves and in others. Social and emotional intelligence is like a compass that guides our interactions, shapes our relationships, and influences our overall well-being.

In today's fast-paced and interconnected world, where relationships and collaborations are fundamental to success, nurturing our social and emotional intelligence is more important than ever. It's not just about being "emotionally intelligent" or "socially adept"—it's about thriving in a world where empathy, resilience, and effective communication are essential skills for navigating life's challenges.

For many in the African American community, the pursuit of success is not just about individual achievement—it's about overcoming systemic barriers, breaking through stereotypes, and uplifting entire communities. In this context, social and emotional intelligence takes on even greater significance. It becomes a powerful tool for resilience, empowerment, and collective progress.

Social and emotional intelligence, or EQ, is more than just a buzzword—it's a set of skills that can empower you to thrive in diverse environments, build meaningful connections, and navigate the complexities of today's world with confidence and authenticity. Whether you're striving for professional success, seeking personal fulfillment, or aiming to effect positive change in your community, nurturing your social and emotional intelligence is essential.

As Oprah Winfrey once said, "Leadership is about empathy. It is about having the ability to relate to and connect with people for the purpose of inspiring and empowering their lives." In this chapter, we'll explore why social and emotional intelligence is essential for our success and growth as members of the African American community. Through practical strategies, inspiring stories, and actionable insights, we'll embark on a journey of self-discovery and empowerment. Together, we'll harness the transformative power of social and emotional intelligence to overcome obstacles, seize opportunities, and build a brighter future for ourselves and those around us. So, let's dive in and discover how cultivating these invaluable skills can propel us toward success, resilience, and lasting impact.

Importance of Social and Emotional Skills:

Empathy, self-awareness, and relationship-building are not just buzzwords thrown around in self-help books—they are the cornerstones of personal and professional success. Let's unpack why these qualities are so crucial in our journey toward fulfillment and achievement.

1. Empathy:

Empathy is the ability to understand and share the feelings of others. In both personal and professional contexts, empathy fosters deeper connections, strengthens relationships, and promotes mutual understanding. When we can step into someone else's shoes and see the world from their perspective, we build trust, foster collaboration, and create a supportive environment where everyone feels valued and heard.

2. Self-Awareness:

Self-awareness is the foundation upon which personal growth and development are built. It involves having a clear understanding of our strengths, weaknesses, values, and emotions. By cultivating self-awareness, we become better equipped to navigate life's challenges, make informed decisions, and pursue goals aligned with our authentic selves. In the professional realm, self-awareness enables us to leverage our strengths, address areas for improvement, and strive for excellence with confidence and clarity.

3. Relationship-Building:

At its core, success is not a solo endeavor—it's a collaborative effort that thrives on meaningful relationships. Whether in the workplace, our communities, or our personal lives, strong relationships are the bedrock of success. Building and nurturing authentic connections fosters trust, fosters teamwork, and opens doors to new opportunities. By investing in relationships based on mutual respect, empathy, and communication, we create a support network that propels us forward and enriches our lives in countless ways.

Maximizing Social and Emotional Skills for Effective Communication

Developing social and emotional skills enriches your communication abilities in multifaceted ways. By refining these skills, you unlock a deeper level of connection and understanding in your interactions with others. Here's how honing social and emotional skills contributes to fostering effective communication:

1. Understanding Others' Perspectives:

Delving into empathy allows you to step into the shoes of others, understanding their feelings, perspectives, and experiences. This heightened empathy fosters genuine connections by signaling to others that you value and respect their emotions and viewpoints. As a result, your communication becomes more inclusive, empathetic, and conducive to meaningful dialogue.

2. Enhancing Self-Reflection:

Embracing self-awareness empowers you to delve into your own thoughts, emotions, and communication patterns. By gaining insights into your strengths, weaknesses, and triggers, you can refine your communication style to align with your authentic self. This introspection enables you to communicate with greater clarity, consistency, and confidence, enhancing the impact of your messages.

3. Navigating Emotional Terrain:

Developing emotional intelligence equips you with the tools to navigate the complex landscape of emotions effectively. By mastering emotional regulation, you can manage your own emotions and responses in challenging situations, maintaining composure and clarity in your communication. Additionally, understanding others' emotions allows you to respond with empathy and sensitivity, fostering trust and rapport in your interactions.

4. Fostering Meaningful Connections:

Prioritizing relationship-building cultivates deeper connections and trust in your personal and professional relationships. Through active listening, genuine engagement, and empathetic communication, you create an environment where individuals feel valued, heard, and understood. This relational approach to communication strengthens bonds, fosters collaboration, and paves the way for constructive dialogue and conflict resolution.

Navigating Decision-Making

1. Leveraging Your Self-Awareness:

Your self-awareness is instrumental in shaping decision-making within the workplace. When you possess a deep understanding of your own strengths, weaknesses, values, and biases, you can make more informed and aligned decisions. By recognizing your personal preferences, tendencies, and blind spots, you can mitigate potential biases that may cloud your judgment. Your self-awareness enables you to approach decision-making with clarity and objectivity, ensuring that your choices align with organizational goals and values.

2. Harnessing Your Emotional Intelligence:

Your emotional intelligence (EI) also significantly influences decision-making in the workplace. EI encompasses your ability to recognize, understand, and manage your own emotions, as well as to perceive and influence the emotions of others. In the context of decision-making, your high EI allows you to assess situations holistically, considering not only the rational aspects but also the emotional implications. You can navigate complex interpersonal dynamics, anticipate reactions, and engage stakeholders effectively. By incorporating emotional considerations into your decision-making process, you foster greater buy-in, collaboration, and alignment among team members.

3. Integration into Your Decision-Making Processes:

Incorporating self-awareness and emotional intelligence into your decision-making processes enriches the quality and outcomes of decisions in the workplace. As you prioritize self-awareness, engage in reflective practices, seeking feedback from peers and mentors to gain insights into your decision-making tendencies.

Similarly, as you cultivate emotional intelligence, leverage your ability to empathize and connect with others to gather diverse perspectives and build consensus around decisions. By fostering a culture that values self-awareness and emotional intelligence, your organization can nurture decision-makers who make choices that are not only rational but also empathetic, inclusive, and aligned with the collective well-being of the team and the organization as a whole.

Developing Social and Emotional Intelligence:

Navigating through challenging situations can be daunting, especially when emotions run high. However, by employing effective strategies to manage and regulate your emotions, you can navigate these circumstances with greater ease and composure. Here are some strategies tailored to help you regulate your emotions in challenging situations:

1. Practice Mindfulness:

Cultivate mindfulness techniques to anchor yourself in the present moment and observe your emotions without judgment. By focusing on your breath or engaging in grounding exercises, you can maintain a sense of calm amidst turmoil and prevent emotions from overwhelming you.

2. Identify Triggers:

Take time to identify the specific triggers that evoke strong emotional responses in you. Whether it's a particular person, situation, or thought pattern, understanding your triggers empowers you to anticipate and prepare for emotional challenges proactively.

3. Utilize Relaxation Techniques:

Incorporate relaxation techniques such as deep breathing, progressive muscle relaxation, or visualization to alleviate stress and tension in challenging moments. These techniques help activate the body's relaxation response, promoting a sense of calm and equilibrium.

4. Engage in Perspective-Taking:

Step into the shoes of others to gain a broader perspective on the situation. By empathizing with different viewpoints, you can cultivate compassion and understanding, which can mitigate intense emotional reactions and foster collaborative problem-solving.

5. Implement Cognitive Restructuring:

Challenge and reframe negative thought patterns that contribute to heightened emotions. Replace irrational or catastrophic thoughts with more balanced and realistic perspectives, allowing you to approach challenges with greater clarity and resilience.

6. Seek Social Support:

Don't hesitate to reach out to trusted friends, family members, or colleagues for support and encouragement during challenging times. Connecting with others can provide validation, perspective, and reassurance, helping you navigate emotional turmoil more effectively.

7. Set Boundaries:

Establish clear boundaries to protect your emotional well-being and prevent yourself from becoming overwhelmed. Learn to say no to additional responsibilities or commitments when you're already feeling stretched thin, prioritizing self-care and balance.

8. Reflect and Learn:

After navigating a challenging situation, take time to reflect on your emotional responses and the effectiveness of your coping strategies. Identify what worked well and areas for improvement, allowing you to refine your emotional regulation skills for future challenges.

Improving active listening skills:

Improving your active listening skills is essential for fostering effective communication and building strong relationships. Here are some practical exercises and techniques to enhance your ability to listen actively:

1. Mindful Listening:

Practice mindful listening by giving your full attention to the speaker without interrupting or formulating responses in your mind. Focus on understanding the speaker's perspective, emotions, and underlying messages.

2. Reflective Listening:

Engage in reflective listening by paraphrasing and summarizing the speaker's message to ensure accurate understanding. Reflect back the speaker's words and emotions, demonstrating empathy and validation.

3. Maintain Eye Contact:

Maintain appropriate eye contact with the speaker to convey attentiveness and respect. Eye contact signals your interest in the conversation and encourages the speaker to continue sharing.

4. Use Nonverbal Cues:

Utilize nonverbal cues such as nodding, smiling, and leaning forward to signal active engagement and encouragement. Nonverbal cues communicate your presence and receptivity to the speaker's message.

5. Avoid Interrupting:

Resist the urge to interrupt or interject with your own thoughts or opinions while the speaker is talking. Allow the speaker to express themselves fully before offering your perspective or response.

6. Ask Clarifying Questions:

Seek clarification by asking open-ended questions that encourage the speaker to elaborate or clarify their points. Avoid leading questions and instead focus on gaining deeper insights into the speaker's thoughts and feelings.

7. Practice Empathetic Listening:

Cultivate empathy by putting yourself in the speaker's shoes and imagining their experiences, emotions, and challenges. Empathetic listening fosters understanding and connection, strengthening interpersonal relationships.

8. Eliminate Distractions:

Minimize distractions and create a conducive listening environment by turning off electronic devices, finding a quiet space, and eliminating background noise. Create a focused and attentive atmosphere that promotes active listening.

9. Take Notes:

Take notes or jot down key points to aid comprehension and retention of information. Note-taking can help reinforce your understanding of the speaker's message and facilitate follow-up discussions.

10. Provide Feedback:

Offer feedback and validation to the speaker to acknowledge their contributions and demonstrate your engagement. Use affirming statements and positive reinforcement to encourage further sharing.

Personal Stories of Growth:

Through the practice of emotional regulation, I've experienced greater overall well-being. By taking the time to listen more and speak less, I've found that I can better handle disappointment or receive sad news with optimism. I've learned to convince my subconscious mind of positive outcomes and to expect the best in every situation. This shift in mindset has led to positive actions, which in turn generate positive results. In the past, I used to worry excessively, but through mindful practices, I've been able to let go of that habit and approach life with a more optimistic outlook.

CHAPTER 7

THE PRACTICE OF MINDFULNESS

In the hustle and bustle of modern life, it's all too easy to get swept away by the relentless tide of responsibilities, deadlines, and distractions. We find ourselves constantly juggling multiple tasks, racing against the clock, and struggling to keep up with the dizzying pace of the world around us. In the midst of this chaos, our minds become cluttered with worries, anxieties, and to-do lists, leaving us feeling overwhelmed, exhausted, and disconnected from ourselves and those around us.

But what if there was a way to break free from this cycle of stress and busyness? What if we could find a refuge of calm amidst the chaos, a sanctuary where we could cultivate peace, clarity, and inner harmony? This is where mindfulness comes in – a simple yet profound practice that has the power to transform our relationship with ourselves and the world around us.

Mindfulness is the art of paying attention to the present moment with openness, curiosity, and acceptance. It invites us to let go of the past and future, and instead, anchor ourselves in the here and now.

By bringing our awareness to the sensations, thoughts, and emotions arising in each moment, we cultivate a deep sense of presence and connection to life as it unfolds.

But mindfulness is more than just a fleeting moment of calm or relaxation – it's a way of being, a way of living with greater intention, authenticity, and compassion. It's about learning to respond to life's challenges with grace and resilience, rather than reacting from a place of fear or habit. It's about cultivating a sense of inner peace and contentment that is not dependent on external circumstances, but arises from within.

In this chapter, we'll explore the many dimensions of mindfulness and how it can enrich every aspect of our lives – from our relationships and work to our physical and mental well-being. We'll learn practical techniques and exercises for integrating mindfulness into our daily routines, and discover how this ancient practice can help us navigate the complexities of the modern world with greater ease and clarity.

Understanding Mindfulness and its importance:

Imagine mindfulness as a soothing balm for your mind and soul, a practice that invites you to step into the sanctuary of the present moment. It's about gently guiding your attention to the here and now, tuning in to the sensations, thoughts, and emotions that arise within you without judgment or resistance.

In simple terms, mindfulness is the art of being fully present in each moment of your life, whether you're sipping your morning coffee, walking in nature, or engaging in a conversation with a loved one. It's about cultivating a deep sense of awareness and acceptance, allowing you to embrace whatever arises with kindness and curiosity.

At its core, mindfulness is about learning to befriend your own mind, to observe your thoughts and feelings with compassion and understanding. It's about letting go of the past and future, and instead, anchoring yourself in the richness of the present moment.

Through mindfulness, you can cultivate greater clarity, peace, and resilience in your life. It offers a pathway to inner healing and transformation, empowering you to navigate life's challenges with grace and equanimity. With practice, you can learn to tap into the deep wellspring of peace and wisdom that lies within you, finding solace and strength in the midst of life's storms.

The importance of Mindfulness:

"Mindfulness is the aware, balanced acceptance of the present experience. It isn't more complicated than that. It is opening to or receiving the present moment, pleasant or unpleasant, just as it is, without either clinging to it or rejecting it." - Sylvia Boorstein

Imagine a moment of pure clarity, where the noise of the world fades away, and you are fully immersed in the richness of the present moment. This is the essence of mindfulness – a practice that invites you to embrace each moment with open arms, just as it is. But why is mindfulness so crucial in today's fast-paced world? Let's explore its profound significance in nurturing your mental well-being, enhancing your relationships, and fostering resilience in the face of life's challenges.

1. Stress Reduction:

In today's fast-paced world, stress has become a pervasive presence in our lives, taking a toll on our physical, mental, and emotional health. Mindfulness provides a powerful antidote to stress, helping to calm the nervous system and reduce the harmful effects of chronic stress on the body and mind.

2. Emotional Regulation:

Mindfulness empowers us to develop greater emotional intelligence, enabling us to recognize, understand, and regulate our emotions more effectively. By cultivating a non-judgmental awareness of our feelings and reactions, we can respond to challenging situations with greater equanimity and resilience.

3. Enhanced Focus and Concentration:

In a world filled with distractions, mindfulness helps sharpen our focus and attention, allowing us to concentrate more fully on the task at hand. By training the mind to stay present and attentive, we can improve our productivity and performance in all areas of life.

4. Improved Relationships:

Mindfulness fosters deeper connection and empathy in our relationships, enabling us to communicate more authentically and empathically with others. By cultivating present-moment awareness and active listening skills, we can forge stronger bonds and resolve conflicts more effectively.

5. Greater Self-Awareness:

Mindfulness invites us to turn inward and explore the landscape of our own minds with curiosity and compassion. Through regular practice, we develop a deeper understanding of ourselves – our thoughts, beliefs, and patterns of behavior – allowing us to make more conscious choices and live in alignment with our values.

Mindfulness Practices:

In today's fast-paced world, where distractions abound and our attention is constantly pulled in a million different directions, finding moments of peace and clarity can feel like a rare luxury.

However, amidst the chaos, mindfulness practices offer a sanctuary – a gentle invitation to pause, breathe, and reconnect with the present moment. But what exactly are mindfulness practices, and how can they benefit you?

Mindfulness practices encompass a wide range of techniques and exercises designed to cultivate present-moment awareness and inner peace. From simple breathing exercises to guided meditations, these practices are accessible to anyone, regardless of age, background, or experience level. By engaging in mindfulness practices, you embark on a journey of self-discovery and transformation, tapping into the profound wisdom and clarity that resides within you.

But the benefits of mindfulness extend far beyond just finding moments of tranquility in your busy life. Research has shown that regular mindfulness practice can lead to a myriad of positive outcomes, including reduced stress, improved focus and concentration, enhanced emotional regulation, and greater overall well-being. Moreover, mindfulness practices can deepen your connection to yourself and others, fostering compassion, empathy, and resilience in the face of life's challenges.

In the hustle and bustle of modern life, stress and distractions can often feel overwhelming, leaving you feeling scattered and drained. But amidst the chaos, mindfulness exercises and meditation techniques offer a sanctuary – a pathway to inner peace and clarity. Here are some simple yet powerful practices to help you reduce stress and enhance focus:

1. Mindful Breathing:

Begin by finding a comfortable seated position and closing your eyes. Take a few deep breaths, allowing your belly to rise and fall with each inhale and exhale. Now, bring your awareness to your breath, noticing the sensation of air entering and leaving your nostrils. As thoughts arise, gently acknowledge them and return your focus to your breath. Continue this practice for a few minutes, allowing yourself to fully immerse in the present moment.

2. Body Scan Meditation:

Find a quiet space where you can lie down comfortably. Close your eyes and take a few deep breaths to center yourself. Now, bring your attention to your body, starting from your toes and gradually moving upward. Notice any areas of tension or discomfort, and as you exhale, imagine releasing that tension with each breath. Continue scanning your body, bringing awareness to each part and allowing yourself to fully relax.

3. Mindful Walking:

Take a break from your daily routine and go for a mindful walk outdoors. As you walk, bring your attention to each step, noticing the sensation of your feet touching the ground. Pay attention to the sights, sounds, and smells around you, allowing yourself to fully immerse in the present moment. If your mind begins to wander, gently guide your focus back to the sensation of walking.

4. Guided Visualization:

Find a quiet space where you can sit comfortably. Close your eyes and take a few deep breaths to center yourself. Now, envision a peaceful and serene place – it could be a beach, a forest, or any place that brings you joy. Imagine yourself fully immersed in this environment, taking in the sights, sounds, and sensations around you. Allow yourself to relax and unwind as you visualize this tranquil scene.

5. Gratitude Journaling:

Take a few moments each day to reflect on the things you're grateful for. Grab a notebook and jot down three things you're thankful for, no matter how big or small. This simple practice can help shift your focus from negativity to positivity, cultivating a greater sense of appreciation for the present moment.

Personal Stories of Mindfulness:

In college and graduate school, I always found myself stressed when facing tests and exams. To cope with this anxiety and stress, I made the decision to enroll in mindfulness classes. Through these classes, I began to pay more attention to the small things in life that we often take for granted. Whether it was the refreshing smell of fresh air, the peaceful ambiance of the woods at night, or simply taking a moment to close my eyes and meditate in a quiet spot, these practices helped me find moments of calm amidst the chaos. Additionally, I started incorporating early morning drives to the water, where I could watch the waves splash and feel a sense of serenity wash over me.

Through mindfulness, I learned the art of balance, which allowed me to organize my day more effectively and tackle tasks one step at a time. I prioritized self-care by incorporating self-affirmations and making time for myself. These healthy tools became invaluable in managing my stress and anxiety, ultimately leading to better control over my emotions and a greater sense of well-being.

EMBRACING YOUR JOURNEY

Welcome to the final chapter of our journey together. Throughout this book, we've explored a wide range of topics, each one offering insights and strategies to empower you on your path to personal and professional success. As we reach the culmination of our exploration, it's important to reflect on the unique challenges and triumphs experienced by the African American community and how our collective journey can inspire meaningful change.

Take a moment to look back on the path we've traveled together. From mastering finances to cultivating resilience and embracing mindfulness, each chapter has provided valuable tools and perspectives tailored to the needs and experiences of the African American community. Consider the lessons learned, the growth experienced, and the opportunities for transformation that lie ahead.

Throughout this book, we've emphasized the importance of resilience, self-awareness, effective communication, and mindfulness in navigating the complexities of life. These core principles are particularly vital for the African American community, which has historically faced systemic barriers and social injustices. By embracing these principles, we empower ourselves to overcome adversity, amplify our voices, and create positive change in our lives and communities.

Now is the time to put our knowledge into action and drive meaningful change. As members of the African American community, we have a rich legacy of resilience, innovation, and collective strength to draw upon. Let us harness the power of our shared history and experiences to advocate for justice, equity, and opportunity for all. Whether it's advocating for financial literacy, promoting mental health awareness, or supporting initiatives for social justice reform, every action we take brings us closer to our shared vision of a more inclusive and equitable society.

As we embark on this journey of personal and collective growth, let us draw inspiration from the stories of resilience and triumph within our community. From civil rights leaders to everyday heroes, countless individuals have overcome adversity and made lasting contributions to our shared history. Let their stories guide us as we navigate the challenges of today and build a brighter future for generations to come.

While our journey together may be coming to an end, our quest for knowledge and empowerment continues. Seek out additional resources, organizations, and community networks that support the advancement and well-being of the African American community.

From mentorship programs to advocacy groups, there are countless opportunities to connect, learn, and grow together.

As we conclude our journey, I urge you to embrace the lessons learned and commit to ongoing personal and collective growth. Together, let us stand united in our pursuit of justice, equity, and opportunity for all. By harnessing the power of resilience, self-awareness, and community, we can create a future where every individual has the opportunity to thrive.

Thank you for joining me on this transformative journey. As we move forward, may we continue to uplift and support one another, celebrate our successes, and navigate life's challenges with courage and grace. Remember, our strength lies in our resilience, our power lies in our unity, and our future is filled with endless possibilities. Let us embrace this moment as a catalyst for positive change and embark on the next chapter of our journey together.

TESTIMONIALS

Wanda Grant – Educator Burke School – An attention grabber – the importance of application and not just simple knowledge – it's not what you know, it's more of what you can do. All this is facilitated in this book. Bernard Jones is to be commended.

Dr. Steve Boykins, DPM – Podiatrist – Very captivating and inspirational – a must read.

Dr. Amy Smith MD Physician – A good read. Mr. Jones is able to articulate well regarding his ability to speak coherently and fluently.

Jim Talton, COO Synergy – A good overview on the importance of financial literacy, being accountable for your money, and using funds to manage lifelong earnings and investments

Dr. Robert Pipkin, Former Superintendent Administrator - Bernie Jones, Jr. does a majestic job justifying the importance of having the necessary tools to make it in this world. He teaches us to ask ourselves the question that pertains to what our why is in life, controlling what we put into our minds and bodies, and seeking knowledge and truth.